Letter to D

*

Letter to D

A Love Story

André Gorz

Translated by Julie Rose

polity

First published in French as *Lettre à D.: Histoire d'un Amour* © Éditions Galilée.

English translation copyright © Julie Rose, 2008

First published in English in 2017

2

Polity Press
65 Bridge Street
Cambridge CB2 1UR, UK.

Polity Press
101 Station Landing
Suite 300
Medford, MA 02155, USA

Ouvrage publié avec le concours du Ministère français de la Culture – Centre national du livre

Published with the assistance of the French Ministry of Culture – National Centre for the Book

ISBN-13: 978-0-7456-4677-0
ISBN-13: 978-1-5095-4397-7 (pb)

A catalogue record for this book is available from the British Library.

Printed and bound in Great Britain by TJ Books Limited

For further information, visit our website: www.politybooks.com

You're 82 years old. You've shrunk six centimetres, you only weigh 45 kilos yet you're still beautiful, graceful and desirable. We've lived together now for 58 years and I love you more than ever. I once more feel a gnawing emptiness in the hollow of my chest that is only filled when your body is pressed next to mine.

I just need to tell you these simple things again before I deal with the issues that have been eating away at me for some time now. Why is there so little of you in what I've written when our union has been the most important thing in my life? Why did I give such a false image of you in *The Traitor*, an image that disfigures you? That book was supposed to show how my commitment to you was the decisive turning point that gave me the will to live. So why doesn't the wonderful love affair we'd begun seven years earlier really come into it? Why don't I say what fascinated me about you? Why did I present you as this pitiful creature 'who didn't know a soul, didn't speak a word of French, would have destroyed herself without me', when you had your circle of friends, were in a Lausanne theatre company and were eagerly awaited back in England by a man determined to marry you?

I didn't really achieve the profound self-analysis I'd intended in writing *The Traitor*. I still need to understand, to clarify so many questions.

I need to piece together the story of our love to appreciate its full meaning. It's what has allowed us to become who we are, living through each other and for each other. I'm writing to you now to understand what my life has been, what our life together has meant.

✳

Our affair began miraculously, love at first sight, more or less. The day we met, you were surrounded by three men trying to show you how to play poker. You had masses of auburn hair and the peaches-and-cream skin and distinctive sweet voice English women often have. You'd only just stepped off the train from England, and all three men were vying for your attention in their very limited English. You were striking, witty and clever, beautiful as a dream. When our eyes met, I thought: 'I don't stand a chance with her'. I found out later that our host had warned you off me: 'He is an *Austrian Jew*. Totally devoid of interest'.

A month later I passed you in the street and watched you go by, fascinated by the way you walked – like a dancer. Then one evening, as luck would have it, I looked down a side street and caught sight of you in the distance. I turned and ran to catch up. You were walking fast. It had snowed and the drizzle had made your hair go curly. Without thinking I'd get anywhere, I suggested we go dancing. You just said, *Oui*, why not. That was October 23, 1947.

My English was clumsy but passable. It had been improved by two American novels I'd just translated for the publishers, Marguerat. That first time we went out, I gathered you'd read a lot, during and after the war: Virginia Woolf, George Eliot, Tolstoy, Plato ...

We talked about British politics, the different currents at the heart of the Labour Party. You were able to tell the difference between what mattered and what didn't in a flash. Faced with a complex problem, you always knew exactly what decision to make. You had unshakeable confidence in the rightness of your judgment. Where did you get your assurance? You, too, had had parents who'd separated. You had left them at an early age, one after the other, and had lived alone those last years of the war, sharing your rations with your cat, Tabby. Finally, you'd left your native land behind to go and explore other worlds. How could an 'Austrian Jew', without a sou to his name, interest you?

I didn't understand. I didn't know what invisible bonds were being woven between us. You didn't like talking about your past. It was only slowly that I came to understand what kind of formative experience made us so close from the start.

We saw each other again. We went dancing again. We saw *Le Diable au corps*, with Gérard Philippe, together. There's a scene in the film where the heroine asks the sommelier to exchange a bottle of wine they've started drinking because, she says, they can taste the cork. We tried the same trick in a dance hall one night, but when the sommelier checked, he challenged our claim. We insisted and he relented, but not without warning us: 'Never set foot here again!'

I had to admire your sangfroid and sheer cheek. I said to myself: 'We're meant to be.'

At the end of our third or fourth date, I finally kissed you.

✳

We were in no hurry. I took your clothes off and bared your body slowly, with great care. I discovered just how magically reality can coincide with the imaginary. You were a miracle, Venus de Milo made flesh. The luminous sheen of your throat cast a glow over your face. I gazed on this miracle of strength and softness for a long while, lost for words. With you, I understood that pleasure is not something you give or take. It's a way of giving yourself and calling forth the gift of self from the other person. We gave ourselves to each other completely.

In the weeks that followed, we saw each other virtually every night. You shared the old battered sofa that I used as a bed. Since it was only 60 centimetres wide, we had to snuggle up tightly together. Apart from the sofa, the only other things in my room were a bookshelf made out of boards and bricks, a huge table cluttered with papers, a chair and an electric heater. You weren't surprised by my monk-like existence. I wasn't surprised you accepted it.

Before I knew you, I'd never spent more than two hours with a girl without getting bored and letting her know it. What captivated me about you was that you opened the door to another world for me. The values that dominated my childhood had no place there. That world enchanted me. I could leave the real world behind and be someone else, without any ties or obligations. With you, I was *elsewhere*, in a foreign place, foreign to myself. You gave me access to another dimension when I'd always rejected any fixed identity and just worn different identities on top of each other, though none of them were mine.

By speaking to you in English, I made *your* language mine. I've continued to talk to you in English right up to this day, even when you answer me in French. For me, English, which I knew mainly through you and through books, was from the start like a private language that preserved our intimacy against the intrusion of the real world, and its prevailing social norms. I felt like I was building a protected and protective world with you.

We could never have come together like this if you'd had a strong sense of belonging, of having roots deep in British culture. But you didn't. When it came to anything British, you kept a critical distance, though that didn't stop you feeling deeply connected to what was familiar to you from childhood. I used to say you were an 'export only', one of those products reserved for export that you can never find in Great Britain itself.

We both became passionate about the outcome of the elections in Great Britain, but that was because what was at stake there was the future of socialism, not of the United Kingdom.

The worst insult anyone could direct at you was to accuse you of taking Britain's side on anything out of a sense of patriotism. I'd have proof of this much later, during the invasion of the Falklands by Argentine forces. An illustrious visitor at the time tried to claim you were taking Britain's side out of patriotism. You retorted tartly that only a moron could fail to see what Argentina was up to. You said it was obviously conducting the war in a bid to restore the fortunes of the militaro-fascist dictatorship and that the victory of the British would finally bring about its collapse.

But I'm getting ahead of myself. In those first weeks, I was delighted by your free and easy attitude towards your culture of origin but also by the substance of that culture as it had been passed on to you when you were little: a certain way of making light of the gravest ordeals, a sense of humility camouflaged as self-deprecating humour and most especially your nursery rhymes, fiercely nonsensical and cleverly rhymed as they are. For instance: 'Three blind mice/See how they run/They all run after the farmer's wife/Who cut off their tails with a carving knife/Did you ever see such fun in your life/As three blind mice?'

I wanted you to tell me about your childhood down to the very last detail. I knew you'd grown up at your godfather's, in a house with a garden by the sea, with your dog, Jock, who used to bury his bones in the flowerbeds and could never find them again afterwards; that your godfather had a wireless set with batteries that had to be recharged every week. I knew you regularly broke the axle of your tricycle riding down the step onto the footpath; that at school you took hold of your pencil in your left hand and sat on both your hands in defiance of the schoolmistress who wanted to force you to write with your right hand. Your godfather, who was quite a powerful figure, told you the teacher was a cretin and went and had words with her. Hearing this story, I understood that seriousness and respect for authority were foreign to you and always would be.

But none of that can account for the invisible bond that made us feel united from the very beginning. It didn't matter how unalike we were, I still felt we had something fundamental in common, a sort of original wound. Earlier I mentioned a 'formative experience': it was the experience of insecurity. The nature of this insecurity was not the same in you as in me. But that didn't matter: for you, as for me, it meant not having an assured place in the world. We'd only ever have the one we carved out for ourselves. We had to come to terms with our autonomy and I'd discover a little further down the track that you were better prepared for that than I was.

✳

You'd lived in insecurity from early childhood. Your mother had married very young. She'd been separated from her husband almost immediately by the war of 1914. After four years, he returned from the war and was classified a disabled ex-serviceman. For several years, he tried to make a go of family life again but it didn't work. Finally, he went off to live in an old soldiers' home.

Your mother was almost as beautiful as you, judging by the photos, and she had a string of relationships with other men. One of these men, who was always presented to you as your godfather, had retired to a pretty town on the coast after a life of roaming the world. You were about four years old when your mother took you to live with him. But they didn't last as a couple, either. Your mother walked out after about two years, leaving you with your godfather, who was very attached to you.

She came back to see you often in the years that followed. But each of her visits ended in bitter wrangling between her and the man you called your 'godfather' but who you knew, in your heart of hearts, was your father. They both tried to make you take their side against the other.

I can imagine your distress and your loneliness. You told yourself that, if this was love, if this was a couple, you'd rather live on your own and never be in love. And as your parents' fights were mainly over money, you told yourself that love had to think nothing of money to be true.

From the age of seven, you knew you couldn't trust any adult. Not your schoolmistress, who your godfather said was a cretin; not your parents, who took you hostage; not the local pastor, who, on one of his visits to your godfather, started ranting against the Jews.

You said to him: 'But Jesus was a Jew!'

'My dear child,' he shot back, 'Jesus was the Son of God.'

You had no place of your own in the world of adults. It was sink or swim for you – you couldn't help but be strong because your whole world was so precarious. I've always felt your strength at the same time as your underlying fragility. I loved your fragility when you weren't afraid to let it show.

We were both children of precariousness and conflict. We were made to protect each other from both. We needed to create together, by being together, the place in the world that we'd originally been denied. But, for that, our love *also* had to be a pact for life.

I've never put all this into words so clearly. I knew it in my heart of hearts and I sensed you knew it. But it took so long for something so obvious to work its way from real life into my thoughts and action; it's been such a long struggle.

We had to part at the end of the year. I'd been separated from my family when I was 16; I was to see them again when I was nearly 25, once the war was over. They'd become as foreign to me as what had once been my country. I'd decided to come back to Lausanne after a few weeks, but you must have been afraid my family would grab me and hang on to me. A friend lent us his apartment for our last two days together. We had a real bed, a kitchen where you cooked a real meal. We went to the station together, without speaking a word. I think now that we should have got engaged right then and there. At that precise moment, I would have been ready for it. On the railway platform, I pulled out of my pocket the gold watch chain that I was supposed to take back to my father and I hung it around your neck.

While I was in Vienna, I had the big salon of the apartment all to myself, with its grand piano, its bookshelves, its paintings. I'd shut myself in there in the morning, then sneak out to explore the ruins of the old town, and only see my family at dinnertime.

I rewrote Chapter Two of the Essay: 'Aesthetic Conversion, Joy and the Beautiful' and read Dos Passos' *Three Soldiers* and *The Concept of Mediation in Hegel's Philosophy*, or I think that was the title. At the end of January, I told my mother I'd be going 'home', to Lausanne, for my birthday.

'But what's keeping you there?' she asked.

I said: 'My room, my books, my friends and a woman I love.'

I'd only sent you a single letter describing Vienna and the closed world of my nearest and dearest, hoping you'd never meet them. That particular day I sent you a telegram: *'Till Saturday dearest'*.

I think you were already in my room when I got home. Anyone could pick the lock with a pocket knife or a hairpin. It was February, and since the little wood stove was out of action, the only way to stay warm was to hop into bed. The intense clarity of the memories I still have tells me how much I loved you, how much we loved each other.

Over the next three months, we thought about getting married. I had objections of principle, ideological objections. I held marriage to be a bourgeois institution; I thought it was a legal formality, one which socially tamed a relationship that, precisely because it was based on love, bound two people through what was the least social thing about them. The legal tie had a tendency, and even the express mission, to take on a life of its own, independent of the experience and feelings of the couple involved. I also said: 'Who's to say that in ten or twenty years time our lifelong pact will correspond with what we want in terms of who we've become?'

Your reply was unanswerable: 'If you join with someone for life in marriage, you share your lives together and you refrain from doing what might divide or damage your marriage. Building your life together as a couple is your common project and you never finish reinforcing it, adapting it, reshaping it to fit changing situations. We will be what we do together.' That was almost pure Sartre.

In May, we finally decided to go ahead, at least for the moment. I sent word to my mother, asking her to forward the necessary documents. She responded by having my handwriting analysed and sending me the graphologist's expert report establishing that we, you and I, were by nature incompatible. I remember May 8. That's the day my mother came to Lausanne. I'd decided we'd go and see her together at her hotel, at four o'clock in the afternoon.

You sat in the hotel lobby while I went to alert my mother. She was stretched out on the bed with a book.

'I've come with Dorine,' I said. 'I want to introduce her to you.'

'Who's Dorine?' my mother asked. 'What's she to me?'

'We're going to get married.'

My mother was aghast. She proceeded to list all the reasons why the marriage was out of the question.

'She's waiting for you downstairs,' I said. 'Don't you want to see her?'

'No.'

'I'll be off then.'

'Come on, we're leaving,' I said to you. 'She doesn't want to see you.'

You had hardly had time to gather your things when my mother, very much the *grande dame*, came down the stairs, calling: 'Dorine, my dear, I'm so happy to meet you at last!'

Your utter lack of affectation, her affected refinement: how proud I was of the way you faced this grande dame putting on airs and graces and bragging about the education she'd given her son! How proud I was of your contempt for the issue of money which was, for my mother, an insurmountable obstacle to our union.

Everything could then have been so simple. The most radiant creature on earth was ready to share her life with me. You had entrée into 'polite society', the uppercrust circles I'd never associated with; my friends envied me; men would turn their heads to look at you whenever we were out walking hand in hand. How come you'd chosen this 'Austrian Jew' who didn't have a sou to his name?

On paper, I could cite Hero and Leandre, Tristan and Isolda, Romeo and Juliette and show how love is the mutual fascination of two individuals based precisely on what is least definable about them, least socialisable, most resistant to the roles and images of themselves that society imposes on them. We could share almost everything because we had almost nothing to start with.

All I had to do was consent to live the life I was living, to love, more than anything, your eyes, your voice, your smell, your lovely tapered fingers, your way of inhabiting your body, for the whole future to open up to us.

Only, this was the thing: you'd provided me with the possibility of getting away from myself and making myself at home in another world. You were like a messenger from that world. With you, I could give my real self a rest. You were part and parcel of that dissolving of reality — myself included — that I'd been working on for seven or eight years through writing. For me, you were the herald out in front who showed me how to put the menacing world on hold. In that world I was a refugee whose existence was not legitimate, whose future never went beyond the three months of a temporary visa. I had no desire to come back to earth. I'd found refuge in a magical experience and I wasn't about to let it get dragged down into reality. As far back as I can remember, I'd always sought not to exist. You've had to work for years on end to get me to accept the fact that I *do* exist. And I really don't think your work is over yet.

There are several other ways of explaining my reluctance to get married. That reluctance may have theoretical, ideological underpinnings that explain it away. But the main reason was what I've just summed up – the fact that I felt safer living with you in our own private world, far from the reality that marriage implies.

And so I took the official steps our marriage required, but only half-heartedly. I should have realised that, in your mind, it had nothing to do with the legalisation or the socialisation of our union. The whole point of it was to show, quite simply, that we were together for good, that I was ready to make this pact for life with you by which each of us promised their loyalty, their devotion and their tender affection to the other. You've always been faithful to the pact. But you weren't sure at that point if I'd know how to remain faithful to it. My reservations, my silences fuelled your doubts. Right up to that summer's day when you told me calmly that you didn't want to wait anymore for me to make up my mind. You could understand that I might not want to settle down with you. In which case you'd rather leave me before our relationship degenerated into fighting and infidelity.

'Men don't know how to end things,' you said. 'Women prefer a clean break.' The best thing, you suggested, would be for us to separate for a month to give me time to decide what I wanted.

I knew then and there that I didn't need any time to think; that if I let you go I'd spend the rest of my life longing for you. You were the first woman I was able to love body and soul, to feel deeply connected to. You were my first true love, to put it simply. If I wasn't capable of loving you for good, I'd never love anyone. I found words I'd never known how to say; words to tell you that I wanted us to be together for as long as we lived.

You left two days later to spend time with friends who had a big country estate in England. You'd stayed with them there just after the war. At that time you'd bottle-fed a baby lamb and, just like in one of your nursery rhymes, it followed you wherever you went. I thought of the happiness animals gave you, of the owner of the estate who was in love with you and convinced you'd agree to marry him after your sojourn 'on the Continent'.

You promised me you'd come back but I wasn't entirely reassured. You could make a go of your life more easily without me than with me. You didn't need anyone to make your way in the world. You had natural authority, a real way with people and a good head for organisation; you had a great sense of humour; you were comfortable and made everyone else feel comfortable in all situations; everyone you came across soon told you their secrets and turned to you for advice. You grasped other people's problems intuitively, with amazing speed, and helped them see clearly into themselves and sort themselves out.

I wrote to you every day care of an ancient war widow who lived in London on one pound a week. You loved her dearly. My letters were full of tenderness. I was aware of needing you if I was to find my way; of not being able to love anyone but you.

You came back towards the end of summer to share my destitution. You slotted in to Lausanne society more easily than I'd ever done. I mainly spent time with members of an association of former arts students. After a few months, your circle of male friends – and admiring female friends – was larger than mine. You were in a theatre company founded by Charles Apothéloz. His troop called itself *Les Faux Nez*, The False Noses, which was the title of a play 'Apoth' had written, based on a script of Sartre's published in *La Revue du cinéma* in 1947. You went to rehearsals for the play and were in three performances in Lausanne and Montreux.

You made much faster progress in French thanks to the theatre rather than to me,

I'm sure. I tried to get you to use a German method that consisted of learning at least thirty pages of a book by heart. We chose Camus' *The Outsider* which starts like this: 'Mother died today. Or maybe yesterday. I received a telegram from the home: 'Mother passed away. Funeral tomorrow. Yours sincerely'. To this day that first page continues to make us laugh whenever we recite it.

In no time at all you were making more money than I was: through English lessons at first, then as secretary to a British writer who'd gone blind. You would read to her, she'd dictate her mail, and in the afternoon you'd take her for a walk for an hour, guiding her by the arm. She paid you, on the black market, obviously, half of what we needed to survive. You started work at eight in the morning and, when you came home for lunch, I'd only just be up out of bed. I'd stay up writing until one o'clock or three o'clock in the morning. You never complained. I'd reached the second volume of the Essay which was supposed to differentiate individual relationships with others according to some essential hierarchy. I had a lot of trouble with love (to which Sartre devoted about thirty pages in *Being and Nothingness*) for no one can explain, philosophically, why you love and want to be loved by a particular person to the exclusion of all others.

At the time, I didn't look for the answer to the question in the experience I was actually going through. I hadn't discovered, as I've just done here, what the basis of our love was. Or that the obsession, at once painful and delicious, with our appetite for our bodies always coincides and is always renewed, however fleetingly – and when I say bodies, I'm not forgetting that 'the soul *is* the body' for Merleau-Ponty as well as for Sartre — goes back to formative experiences that have their roots deep in childhood. It goes back to the initial, original discovery of the emotions that a voice, a smell, a skin colour, a way of moving and being, which will forever be the ideal norm can set resonating in me. That's it: being passionately in love is a way of resonating with the other, body and soul, and with her or him alone. We are somewhat short of and way beyond philosophy here.

✳

Our years of living hand to mouth ended temporarily in the summer of 1949. Because we both campaigned for Citizens of the World, and hawked their paper on the streets of Lausanne, the international secretary, René Bovard, who'd done time as a conscientious objector, proposed that I become his secretary in Paris: the secretary of the secretary. For the first time in my life, I was formally hired and paid a regular salary.

We discovered Paris together, you and I. Then, and in all the jobs I've had since, you took on your share of the work I had to do. You often came to the office to help open and sort the thousands of letters lying around unanswered. You helped draft circulars in English. We made friends with the foreigners who came to visit the office and would take them out to lunch. We were no longer united only in our private life, but also by joint action in the public sphere.

Except that at ten o'clock at night I'd work on the Essay again until two or three in the morning. 'Come to bed,' you'd say after about three. I'd answer: 'I am coming' and you: 'Don't be coming, come!' There was never any reproach in your voice. I loved you for clamouring for me while leaving me all the time I needed.

You'd married someone, you said, who couldn't live without writing and you knew that a person who wanted to be a writer needs to be able to shut themselves away in seclusion, to make notes at any hour of the day or night; that their work with language goes on well after they've laid down their pen and can take complete possession of them without warning, in the middle of a meal or a conversation.

'If only I knew what was going through your mind,' you'd sometimes say, faced with my long dreamy silences.

But you did know, from having gone through it yourself: a flow of words seeking their most crystal-clear order; snatches of sentences being endlessly reworked; ideas dawning then threatening to evaporate if a code word or a symbol didn't swiftly fix them in memory. To love a writer is to love him writing, you said. 'So, write!'

Little did we know I'd need another six years to finish the Essay. Would I have stuck with it if I'd known? 'I'm sure you would have,' you say. It's not *what* you write that's the essential thing for a writer. Your essential need is to write. To write means taking leave of the world and of yourself in order to turn both yourself and the world into potential material for literary compositions. It's only secondarily that the 'subject' dealt with comes into play. The subject is the necessary condition, but it is incidental to the process of writing. Any subject is right if it allows writing.

For six years, up to 1946, I kept a 'diary'. I wrote to ward off angst. I wrote anything that came into my head. I was a note-maker. A note-maker becomes a writer when his or her need to write is sustained by a subject that allows, in fact demands, that this need be organised into a project.

There are millions of us who spend our lives writing without ever finishing or publishing anything. You yourself went through that. You knew, from the start, that you'd have to protect my writing indefinitely.

✳

We were married at the beginning of autumn, 1949. It never occurred to us to ask for the leave we were entitled to. I think my salary was undeclared. We put aside whatever we earned above the minimum wage in a special savings account, convinced of the precariousness of my job at Citizens of the World.

When, in the spring of 1950, Citizens of the World showed me the door, all you said was: 'We'll manage perfectly well without them'. You faced up to a long year of material hardship almost with glee. You were the rock on which we could build our life as a couple. I don't know how you did it but you managed to rustle up all kinds of odd jobs. You posed as a model at the Grande Chaumière of a morning. An amateur painter, a retired insurance agent, got you to sit for two hours every day so he could do your portrait. You found students for your English lessons. An Italian we'd helped out when we were in Citizens of the World hired you along with five or six others to collect old papers.

You organised week-long visits for groups of English schoolboys and acted as their guide. They were always amazed to discover, at the *Invalides*, the way France worshipped Napoleon. For them, the man was just a dictator who'd been defeated by Wellington and deported to a British island. You set them straight. Several teachers and schoolboys continued to write to you for years. You threw yourself into everything you did. Living hand to mouth gave you wings. It made me, on the other hand, go into a dark depression.

Was it at that point, or before, or after? It was summer, anyway; we were admiring the aerial acrobatics of the swallows in the courtyard of our apartment block and you said: 'So much freedom for so little responsibility!' At lunch, you said: 'Do you know you haven't said a word to me for three days?' I wonder if you didn't feel more alone with me than if you'd lived on your own.

I never told you at the time the reasons why I was feeling so bleak. I would've been ashamed to. I admired your assurance, your confidence in the future, your ability to seize whatever moments of happiness came along. I loved the fact that one day you had lunch with Betty eating only black cherries from a big paper cone in the square in the middle of Saint-Germain. You had more friends than I did. For me, hardship had a harrowing face. I only had a temporary resident's visa and, to get it extended, I had to have a job. I went out to Pantin where a chemical plant was looking for an archivist-translator but I was over-qualified for that job. I went and sat through a recruiting session for insurance agents, but the work consisted of going door-knocking and hammering the poor residents with some spiel designed to force them into signing a contract. Thanks to Sartre's intervention, I got Marcel Duhamel to let me translate a detective novel, but that only represented six weeks' work, without any follow-up.

I sat for a test at UNESCO as a German translator and came second out of about thirty candidates. I'd cart myself off to UNESCO every month to see if there was any position vacant, it didn't matter what. But there never was. I discovered you can't get anywhere without 'connections', but we didn't have any. I had no real contacts in the intellectual world and there was no one with whom I could talk over the philosophical ideas my imagination was teeming with in those days. I was staring at failure. Your confidence consoled me but didn't make me feel any safer. In the end, thanks to making myself known at UNESCO, I landed a temporary job at the Indian Embassy, as secretary to the military attaché there. I gave two-hour lessons every day to the attaché's daughters and then drew up reports on the balance of forces in Europe, reports he'd then send off, just as they were, to his home government. That at least allowed me to exercise some of my talents. I had the feeling I wasn't worthy of you; that you deserved better.

✳

Those days of living hand to mouth came to an end in spring, 1951. Thanks to a famous journalist an American friend named Jane introduced us to, I found work that seemed tailor-made for me: I was to edit a new one-page round-up of the foreign press for a daily evening paper, *Paris-Presse*. The editorial office was in a crumbling apartment building in the rue du Croissant, right next to the café where Jean Jaurès was assassinated.

Every day the 'revue de presse' received about forty newspapers or weeklies: all the British publications, from the most serious to the most frivolous; all the American weeklies, plus three dailies whose two kilos of paper fuelled the little metal stove that heated our one-room apartment; plus the German, Swiss,

Belgian press and two Italian dailies. There were only two of us journalists there to mine this mass of information. So I swiftly became the chief editor of the service. You often came in to the office to go through a good part of the English-language publications, cutting out and classifying feature articles. Your elegance and your British sense of humour caused my stocks to rise with the bosses. I accumulated a journalist's encyclopaedic knowledge on just about every country and every issue, including technoscientific, medical and military issues. Thanks to the dozens of files that you fed me day after day, in one night I could write a whole page of the paper on just about anything and everything.

Over the next thirty years, you continued to keep up to date, to expand and manage the material you began amassing in

1951. It followed me to *L'Express* in 1955 and to the *Nouvel Observateur* in 1964. My subsequent employers knew that I couldn't do without you.

Our married life had never been as full and vibrant as it became after I joined the paper. We complemented each other. On top of the press roundup, which was a full-time job, I was employed part-time on the foreign desk. I was perfectly 'in my element' in that job: it consisted of putting myself somewhere else, of attending exclusively to what was foreign to my circle and to the public for whom I wrote; of making myself absent. I looked at the world through foreign eyes, learned to step aside and let the facts come to the fore, to let them speak for themselves, without putting myself in the picture. I learned the tricks of objectivity, in other words. I was in my proper place by dint of not being there. From that point on the Essay only monopolised me from ten o'clock at night until midnight and at weekends.

It would've been quite a happy time if we hadn't had to leave the room in the rue des Saints-Pères that a friend, a woman we'd met in Lausanne, had lent us for three years. The best we could come up with was two little attic rooms separated by the landing in an apartment block in the eleventh arrondissement. Up until then, we'd lived in poverty but never in ugliness. We discovered that you're worse off in the rue Saint-Maur than in Saint-Germain-des-Prés, even if you're making more money.

You felt personally like you were in exile in that part of town. When you didn't come in to the paper, you were lonely, cut-off.

You didn't see your friends nearly as often, now that they were a good half-hour away by metro. Whenever you left the house, wherever you went, there was nothing but deserted streets, dusty shops. You became sad.

＊

After two or three years living in exile like this, life took a turn for the better. I was hired by *L'Express*. The research material you'd compiled had been a real asset in landing the job. I remember exactly how it happened.

L'Express had become a daily designed to support Pierre Mendès France's electoral campaign of 1955-56. When the paper went back to being a weekly again, the journalists on the daily, of which I was one, were told they'd be sacked unless they could prove themselves in the first issues of the new format. I remember writing a feature on peaceful coexistence, quoting a speech of Eisenhower's from three years earlier outlining all that brought the American and Soviet peoples together. At the time no one had bylines at *L'Express*. JJSS, as we called Jean-Jacques Servan-Schreiber, cited mine as a perfect example of the kind of thing he was looking for and ended on this note: 'Here's a person who knows the value of solid source material'.

We acquired, you and I, a reputation for being inseparable, 'obsessionally concerned for each other', Jean Daniel would later write. I managed to finish the Essay in the course of those same weeks and a few days later we found a small rundown apartment in the rue du Bac at an amazingly low price. All we'd hoped for was about to happen.

*

I've described elsewhere the reception Sartre gave the staggering mass of pages I foisted on him. I realised then what I'd known from the start: that manuscript was never going to find a publisher, even if Sartre recommended it ('You over-estimate my power,' he said).

You saw how badly I took it, then the way I blindly refused to come to terms with the problem: I began writing a devastating attack on myself that was to become the start of a new book.

I wondered how you could bear the fact that work I'd subordinated everything else to for as long as you'd known me had ended in failure. And here I was, trying to get over it by launching myself head first into a new venture that was going to monopolise me for God knows how long. But you didn't seem worried or even annoyed. 'Your life is writing. So, write,' you said again. As though your vocation was to comfort me in mine.

Our life changed. People flocked to our little apartment. You had your regular friends who'd drop in at the end of the day for a whisky. You organised dinners or lunches several times a week. We lived at the centre of the universe. For us, the distinction between contacts, information-gatherers and friends became blurred. Branko, a Yugoslav diplomat, was all those things at once. He started out as the head of the Yugoslav Information Centre in the avenue de l'Opéra and ended up as first secretary at the embassy.

Thanks to Branko, we met certain French and foreign intellectuals who were dominant figures in the postwar period.

You had your own circle, your own life, even while you were completely involved in mine. At our first New Year's Eve with 'Castor', Sartre and the *Temps modernes* 'family', Sartre set about seducing you with earnest intensity and the jubilation shone on his face when you responded with the breezy irreverence you reserved for the great of this world. I don't know whether it was on that occasion or later that one of Sartre's friends put me seriously on my guard: 'My dear G., watch out. Your wife's more beautiful than ever. If I decide to go after her, I'll be ir-re-sis-tible.'

It was in the rue du Bac that you really came into your own. You traded that sweet little English voice of yours (the voice that Jane Birkin, among others, has never ceased cultivating) for a good steady deep voice. You lopped off some of that magnificent head of hair of yours that I used to love burying my face in. You kept only a hint of an English accent. You read Beckett, Sarraute, Butor, Calvino, Pavese. You followed Claude Lévi-Strauss' lectures at the Collège de France. You wanted to learn German and bought yourself the requisite books. I stopped you. 'I don't want you to learn a single word of that language,' I told you. 'I'll never speak German again.' You could understand that attitude on the part of an 'Austrian Jew'.

We did nearly all my assignments in France and abroad together. You made me see my limits. I've never forgotten the lesson I learned those three days we spent in Grenoble with Mendès France. It was one of our very first assignments. We ate our meals with Mendès, visited his friends with him, sat in on his interviews with the town worthies. You knew that, parallel to these interviews, I was going to hold talks with trade union militants from the CFDT, *Confédération française démocratique due travail,* for whom the big bosses of Grenoble did not exactly embody 'the lifeblood of the nation', in Mendès' phrase. You absolutely insisted that Mendès read my 'report' before I sent it off. He was grateful you did. 'If you publish that,' he told me, 'I'll never be able to set foot in this town again.' He seemed more amused than annoyed; as though he thought it was only normal that at my age and in my position I should prefer radicalism to any sense of political reality.

I realised that day that you had more of a feel for politics than I did. You picked up realities that escaped me if they failed to correspond with my view of the real world. I became a bit more humble. I got into the habit of getting you to read my articles and manuscripts before filing them. I took your criticisms into account, though I always grumbled: 'Why do you always have to be right!'

The foundation on which our marriage was based changed over those years. Our relationship became the filter that my connection to reality passed through. A shift occurred in our relationship. For a long time you'd let yourself be intimidated by my intellectual arrogance; you felt that was my way of showing a grasp of theory that you couldn't match. Little by little, you refused to let yourself be swayed. Better yet: you rebelled against theoretical constructs and especially against statistics. Statistics as a discipline was even less convincing, you said, than theory, as figures only made sense when they were interpreted. You argued that such interpretation can't lay claim to the mathematical rigour statistics bases its authority on. I needed theory to structure my thinking and I used to object that unstructured thought always runs the risk of degenerating into insignificant, empirical anecdote. You replied that theory always runs the risk of blinding us to the shifting complexities of the real world.

We had these discussions dozens of times and knew in advance what the other was going to come back with. In the end it was all just a game. But even if it was just a game, you were right and I was wrong. You didn't need the cognitive sciences to know that without intuition or emotion, there can be no intelligence or meaning. You based the certainty of your opinions, imperturbably, on lived experience, which can be communicated but not demonstrated. The authority – let's call it ethical – of such opinions does not require debate to hold sway. Whereas the authority of a theoretical opinion collapses if it can't convince through debate. That was precisely the point of my 'Why do you always have to be right!'. I think I needed your judgment more than you needed mine.

✳

Our rue du Bac days lasted ten years. I don't want to retrace those years here but to get a clear sense of where we were headed. We were doing more and more together and, at the same time, seeing ourselves more and more as distinct people, separate from each other. This trend would continue. You'd always been more grown up than I was and became even more so. You liked to say you saw a child's 'innocence' in my eyes; you could well have said 'naïveté'. You were flourishing without doctrines, theories and systems of thought. I needed those psychological crutches to position myself in the intellectual world, even if it meant kicking them out from under me, so to speak. It was in the rue du Bac that I wrote three quarters of *The Traitor* and the three essays that followed.

The Traitor came out in 1958, eighteen months after I handed in the manuscript. Barely 24 hours after I'd dropped it off at du Seuil, you got a phone call from Francis Jeanson. He asked you: 'What's he doing now?'

'He hasn't stopped writing,' you told him. You realised that Jeanson had decided to publish the manuscript.

You've often said that that book transformed me as I wrote it. 'When you finished it, you weren't the same'. I think you were wrong about that. It wasn't writing it that allowed me to change; it was producing a text that was publishable and then seeing it published. Its publication changed my situation. It gave me a place in the world, it gave what I thought reality, a reality that exceeded my intentions, that forced me to redefine myself and to constantly surpass myself so that I wouldn't become trapped either by the image other people had of me or by a product that had turned into something other than me through its objective reality. That's the magic of literature: it gave me access to existence. By writing about my refusal to exist, I described, *wrote*, myself into existence. That book was the product of my refusal, was this refusal and yet, by being published, prevented me from persisting in this refusal. That's precisely what I'd hoped for and nothing other than being published would allow me to achieve: to be forced to commit myself in a way I couldn't do on my own and to ask myself questions, to pursue ends that I hadn't defined on my own either.

So, the book had an impact, but not through the work I did writing it. It gradually had an impact just by confronting me with possibilities and relationships with other people I hadn't initially anticipated. It had an impact, it seems to me, in 1959, when JJSS discovered I had skills in political economics: I no longer had to stick to matters *foreign*. The act of writing can become bogged down by the way others see you as well as by the weight of material realities. *Le Vieillissement, Aging*, was to be my farewell to adolescence, my renunciation of what Deleuze and Guattari were to call 'the limitlessness of desire' and what Georges Bataille called 'the omnitude of possibility' that you only approach by indefinite refusal of all determination: the desire to be Nothing blurs into the desire to be Everything. At the end of *Aging,* this exhortation occurs, directed at myself: 'You have to accept being finite: being here and nowhere else, doing this and not something else, now and not always or never … having only this life.'

✳

Up to 1958 or 1959, I was aware that in writing *The Traitor* I hadn't shed my desire 'to be Nothing, nobody, wholly buried within myself, not objectifiable and not identifiable'. Aware enough to note that 'this meditation about myself confirmed and necessarily prolonged my fundamental choice [of nonexistence] and so I couldn't hope to revise that choice.' And this was not only because it didn't commit me, but also because *I* did not really commit *myself* to it. I'd adopted the stand of writing in the third person to avoid complicity with – complacency towards – myself. The third person kept me at a distance from myself, it allowed me to draw, in a neutral language, fuelled by code, a quasi-clinical portrait of the way I was and the way I operated. That portrait was often fierce and full of derision. I avoided the trap of complacency only to fall into that other trap: wallowing in the ferocity of self-criticism. I was that pure invisible eye, completely detached from what it sees. I transformed what I managed to understand of me into knowledge of me and, in so doing, never coincided with this me that I knew as Other. That essay never stopped saying: 'See, I am better than who I am.' I need to explain all this to you because this attitude explains so many things.

I only skimmed the proofs of *The Traitor*. I've never reread any of these texts of mine that turned into books. I hate the expression 'my book': for me it crystallises the peculiar vanity that makes a subject deck himself out in qualities others bestow on him but only insofar as he is himself an Other. The book is no longer 'my thinking' since it's become an object, bang in the middle of a world that belongs to others and escapes me. With *The Traitor*, the last thing I wanted was 'to write a book'. I didn't want to deliver the results of research but to write up the research itself, as it was actually being carried out, with its nascent discoveries, its misses, its wrong tracks, its groping elaboration of a method that never gets finalised. Aware that, 'when everything's said, everything remains to be said, everything always remains to be said'. In other words: it's the *saying* that matters, not the *said*. What I'd written interested me a lot less than what I might write next. I think this is true for any writer, published or otherwise.

The research in fact stops at the second chapter. From before the third, I know only too well what I'm going to find and how I'm going to conclude. Maurice Blanchot noted this in a long article: all the conclusion (the 'I' chapter) does is give a coherent, rounded form to the argument already presented in the first chapter. It offers no discovery. The third and fourth chapters are overrun with themes and reflections that act like a prelude to the next work, which develops them.

The chapter titled 'You', overloaded with digressions as it is, bore the brunt of this – as I discovered to my dismay after *The Traitor* came out in Folio. I'd barely glanced at the proofs, except to put back the nine or ten pages of cuts I'd made in the chapter titled 'You' twenty years earlier for the English version published by Verso. These cuts especially concerned an argument with Romain Rolland and an enormous 'footnote' covering four full pages in tiny print. I'd slipped in this digression on philosophy and revolution between spelling out '[my] way of reducing any personal conflict to a general illustration of Conflict', and of 'taking refuge in the realm of ideas where all things are merely incidental illustrations of a general idea'. Condemning this attitude in no way prevented me from persevering with it. The chapter that follows 'You' offers almost comic examples of this.

This chapter – the 'I' chapter – was supposed to mark the major turning point in my life. It was supposed to show how my love for you or, more to the point, the discovery with you of love, was finally to bring me to want to exist; and how my commitment to you was what would motivate me to change my whole life. So the tale stops eight years before the writing of *The Traitor*, with the vow never to let myself be parted from you. The 'program' is then fulfilled. Pause in the organ music. I then completely change the subject, describe the central role money plays in capitalist society, attack the capitalist consumer model and way of life, and so on – all things that would be dealt with in the following book.

The trouble is that there's no trace of any life-changing existential epiphany in this chapter; no trace of my, of our, discovery of love, of our affair. My vow remains a formality. I don't really come to terms with it, don't flesh it out. On the contrary, I flail about vainly trying to justify it in the name of universal principles, as though I was ashamed of it. Though I have enough insight to note: 'Isn't it obvious that I talked about

Kay as though I was talking about some weakness and in an apologetic tone of excuse, as if a person had to apologise for living?'

So what is it that motivates me in this chapter – in the whole book, for that matter? Why do I talk about you in this dismissive, condescending way? Why, in the tiny space I give you, are you mutilated, totally misrepresented, humiliated? And why are these allusive threads of our affair woven through with another affair – one that's doomed to failure, one that I can't wait to break off yet take pleasure in analysing at length? I asked myself these questions with dismay on rereading the words I wrote. What motivates me, above all, is an obsessive need to elevate myself above what I experience, feel and think, in order to theorise it, to intellectualise it, to be nothing but pure transparent intellect.

That was already the motivation throughout the Essay. It's more immediately obvious here. I refer to you as the only woman I've ever really loved and to our union as the most important decision in both our lives. But evidently that story doesn't inspire me to want to write about it, and neither do the seven years that, at the time I was writing *The Traitor*, had gone by since we made the decision to get married. Being passionately in love for the first time, being loved in return – this was apparently too banal, too private, too *common*: it wasn't the kind of material that would allow me to rise to the universal. A love affair that's hit the rocks, that can never be – now that, on the other hand, makes for high literature. I'm comfortable with the art of failure and annihilation, not with the art of success and positive affirmation. I have to elevate myself above me and you, at our expense, at your expense, through considerations that go beyond us as specific individuals.

The object of the chapter is to condemn this attitude, to show how it brought us to the brink of ending the relationship and going our separate ways; and how, if I didn't want to lose you, I had to choose: either to live without you according to my abstract principles, or to disentangle myself from those principles to live with you: '... He chose Kay over the principles; but grudgingly and without even realising' the very real sacrifices – not ones of principle – that you chose to make.

The tale of what I present as a life-changing experience is then poisoned by eleven lines that belie it. I describe myself perfectly accurately as I was in that spring of 1948: unbearable. 'After they'd started living together in a six square metre hole ... he came and went without saying a word, spent his days on his papers and answered [Kay] in impatient monosyllables. 'You're all you need,' she'd say. It's true that there was no room for anyone in particular in his life ... because, as a particular individual, he did not count and so it could be of no concern to him whether anyone became attached to him as a particular individual.'

A whole page follows of what I myself describe as 'a pretentious dissertation on love and marriage'.

I sound like I'm judging who I was rather harshly. But why, in this page and a half written seven years later, in 1955 or 1956, are there six lines that refer to you as this pitiful girl who 'didn't know a soul', 'didn't speak a word of French' – after six months in Switzerland? Yet I knew you had your circle of friends, made a better living than I did, were expected back in England by a faithful friend and admirer absolutely determined to marry you. Why, then, these hateful lines: 'Kay who, one way or another ... would have destroyed herself if he'd dropped her ...'

Nine pages further on, in the tale of my 'vow', there are another five lines of poison. You'd told me – and, given my casual manner, it came as no surprise – that 'if we're only going to be together for a little while [you'd] prefer to leave now and take the memory of our love away with you intact'. I acknowledge the blow, but only by once more presenting a pitiful image of you: '... If he let Kay go, knowing all his life that she was trailing the memory of him around somewhere ... seeking refuge in her devotion to the sick or her duty of care to a family ... he would be a traitor and a coward. And then, if he wasn't sure he'd be able to live with her, he was sure he didn't want to lose her. He pressed Kay to him and said, with a sense of relief, as though freed at last: "If you go, I'll follow you. I couldn't bear to have let you go." And after a moment he added: "Ever".'

In reality, what I said at that moment was: 'I love you'. But that doesn't feature in the tale.

So why do I seem so sure that our separation would be more unbearable for you than for me? To avoid having to admit the opposite? Why do I say that I was responsible 'for the turn [your] life would take? That it was up to me "to make [your] life livable?"' In all, eleven lines of poison in three doses, over twenty pages; three tiny strokes that debase you and distort you, written seven years later, that rob us of the meaning of seven years of our life.

Who wrote those eleven lines? I mean: Who was I when I wrote those lines? I feel a painful need to give us back those seven years along with what you truly meant to me. I've already tried, here, to give us back great sweeps of the story of our love affair and our marriage. I haven't yet explored the period in which I wrote those pages. That's where I need to look for explanations. I remember that 1955 was a relatively happy year. I was about to change jobs and work for a different paper. We spent our holidays on the shores of the Atlantic. I began *The Traitor* in the eleventh arrondissement, racked with angst. The last day of the year, we signed the contract for the rue du Bac. We had months of happiness and hope after that.

But, the more headway I made on it, the more the manuscript became loaded with political considerations. The chapter 'You' doggedly views personal, private relationships, including relationships based on love and the couple, in the context of alienating social relationships. Gide notes somewhere in his *Diary* that he always feels the need to oppose what he's just written in the next work. That was also the case with me. Exploring myself was literally a dead-end. You can't do it twice.

I was already gearing up for the next work, even if it was still only hazily defined, by reading Jean-Yves Calvez's *Marx*, the writings of the young Marx and Isaac Deutscher's *Stalin*. I thought Kruschev's report to the Twentieth Congress marked a critical turning point, that intellectuals were going to be able to play a decisive role in the communist movement. I was starting to act like one of the members of a theatre company described by Kazimierz Brandys in *The Defence of Grenada* who want to conform completely to the directives of the Party but suspect themselves, and everyone else, of harbouring secret reservations about their task. I wasn't far off considering love to be a petit-bourgeois sentiment.

I 'talked about you in an apologetic tone of excuse, as though I was talking about some weakness' (this remark in *The Traitor* now takes on its full significance: obviously it was your attachment to me that I felt was a weakness – in what I wrote, at least). At the time François Erval said to me one day: 'You have a real revolutionist fixation.' You watched this pro-communist development of mine with anxiety and, at times, anger. At the same time, you made me love the opening up of our private space, of our married life. A note of Kafka's in his *Diary* sums up my state of mind then: 'My love for you doesn't like itself'. I didn't like myself for loving you.

I finally understood that I couldn't commit myself to the communist cause except for the wrong reasons and that intellectuals could not, not for a long time to come, power a transformation of the PCF, the *Parti communiste français*. The new acquaintances we made early in 1957 certainly helped me move on, as well as new reading: notably David Riesman and C. Wright Mills.

When *The Traitor* came out at last, I became conscious once more of what I owed you: you gave all of yourself to help me become myself. The dedication I wrote in your copy said: 'To you, alias Kay, who, in giving me You, have given me I.'

If only I'd developed that in what has become 'my book'.

✳

I have to step back a bit now to tackle the next phase of our story. During our rue du Bac years, we gradually achieved relative financial security. But we never spent anything like what we could have spent on our standard of living or level of consumption. There was a tacit agreement between us on that score. We had the same values, by which I mean the same conception of what gives life meaning or threatens to take it away. As far back as I can remember, I've always hated the so-called 'good life' and its squandering. You refused to follow the fashion and had your own ideas about what to wear. You refused to let advertising or marketing supply you with needs you didn't feel. On holidays, we'd stay either 'with a family' in Spain, or in modest hostels or guesthouses in Italy. It wasn't until 1968 that we went to a big modern hotel, for the first time – in Pugnochiuso. We ended up acquiring an old Austin after ten years. That didn't stop us considering individual car ownership to be a disastrous political choice that pits individuals against each other by claiming to offer them the means of escaping the common lot. For household expenses you had a budget that you set and managed according to our needs. This reminds me how you'd decided, at the age of seven, that to be true, love must think nothing of money. You thought nothing of it. We often gave it away.

We got into the habit of spending our weekends in the country. Then, so we didn't have to stay at a guesthouse, we bought a cottage 50 kilometres from Paris. We'd go for two-hour walks in all weather. You had a natural affinity with all living things that was contagious and you taught me how to look at and love the countryside, the woods, animals. Animals listened to you so intently when you talked to them I had the impression they understood what you were saying. You opened up the richness of life for me and I loved life through you – unless it was the reverse and I loved you through all living things (but that comes down to the same thing). Just after we moved to the cottage you adopted a grey tabby cat, visibly starving, who was always waiting at our front door. We cured him of mange. The first time he jumped on my knees unbidden, I had the feeling he was doing me a great honour.

Our ethic – if I can call it that – primed us to greet May '68 and what followed with jubilation. From the first, we preferred VLR, *Vive La Révolution*, to GP, *Gauche prolétarienne*, Tiennot Grumbach and his militant community at Mantes to Benny Lévy and *La Cause du peuple*. Abroad, I passed for a precursor and even an instigator of the May movements. We went together to Belgium, the Netherlands, England, then in 1970 to Cambridge, Massachusetts.

Five years earlier in New York, we'd hated the so-called American dream with its wastefulness, its smog, its 'French' fries with ketchup and Coca-Cola, the brutality and the infernal pace of its urban life. We had no idea that Paris would soon be spared none of that. In Cambridge, we were won over by our hosts' hospitality and their passion for new ideas. We discovered a sort of counter-society beavering away, digging its tunnels under the crust of the society on show, waiting for the right moment to emerge into the light of day. We'd never seen so many 'existentialists' — people determined to 'change their lives' by undertaking to live together differently and put their alternative aspirations into practice, without expecting anything from the political powers in place. We were invited to Washington by a think tank. You were invited to several gatherings of Bread and Roses and persuaded them to let me come, too. When we returned to Paris, you brought back several new books, including *Our Bodies, Our Selves*. We shared a world but we looked at it from different angles. Those differences made us rich.

That trip to the United States was a real boost generally and spurred our interest in other issues and ideas. It helped me understand that the classic forms and objectives of class struggle can't change society, that the trade union struggle had to shift to new ground. The following summer, we got very excited about a certain essay. It was a draft of the keynote address to be delivered at a seminar in Cuernavaca, Mexico. I don't know how Jean Daniel got his hands on this draft. He asked me to paraphrase it for the journal. The provisional title was *Retooling Society*. It started by asserting that the pursuit of economic growth was going to lead to multiple disasters that would threaten human life in eight ways. There were echoes of the thinking of Jacques Ellul and Günther Anders in there: the expansion of industry transforms society into a gigantic machine which, instead of liberating human beings, restricts their autonomy, determining the ends they are to pursue and how they are to pursue them. We become servants of this megamachine. Production is no longer at our service, we are at the service of production. And as a result of the simultaneous professionalisation of services of every stripe, we become incapable of taking charge of ourselves, of determining our needs and satisfying them ourselves: we depend in all things on 'incapacitating professions'.

We discussed this essay over the summer holidays. It was signed 'Ivan Illich'. It placed the notion of 'self-management', which was in vogue throughout the Left, in a new light. It confirmed the urgency of 'technocriticism', of retooling the techniques of production. We'd met a protagonist of technocriticism at Harvard. It legitimised our need to broaden the sphere of our autonomy, to not think of autonomy as a private need only. It probably played a role in our project of building a real house of our own. You sketched the layout over those summer holidays: a house shaped like a 'U'.

So, together we entered an era of what was to become political ecology. It looked to us like an extension of the ideas and movements of 1968. We saw a lot of Michel Rolant and Robert Laponche, the people from *La Gueule ouverte* and *Sauvage*, in search of a new direction in technoscience, energy policy and our whole way of living.

We met Illich for the first time in 1973. He wanted to invite us to a seminar on medicine planned for the following year. We had no inkling that the critique of techno-medicine was soon to coincide with our personal concerns.

In 1973, you were working at Éditions Galilée setting up a foreign rights department, which you ended up running for three years. On weekends, we'd go for picnics at the worksite of our future house. We were united in everything. But your life was spoiled by unexplained cramps and headaches. Your physiotherapist suspected that it might be due to you being highly-strung. Your doctor examined you but couldn't find anything and so prescribed tranquillisers. The tranquillisers depressed you to the point where, to your own amazement, you were sometimes in floods of tears. You've never taken any again since.

We went to Cuernavaca the following summer. There I studied the research material that Illich had put together for his book, *Medical Nemesis*. It was agreed I'd do some articles when the book came out. The first article was titled 'When medicine makes you sick'. Today most people would say it merely stated the obvious. At the time, only three letters from doctors supported it; the rest attacked it. One of the supportive letters was signed 'Court-Payen'. His letter stressed the difference between a syndrome and a disease and defended a holistic view of health.

I went to see the good Dr Court-Payen when your state of health deteriorated dramatically. You could no longer lie down, your head hurt so much. You'd spend the night standing on the balcony or sitting in an armchair. I'd wanted to believe that we were together in everything, but you were alone in your distress.

※

On the X-ray he did of your spine and head, Dr Court-Payen noted the presence of lumps of a substance used in X-rays to provide contrast, spread through the spinal canal, from the lumbar vertebrae right up to your head. This dye, lipidiol, had been injected into you eight years earlier, before you were operated on for a paralysing slipped disc. I heard the radiologist reassure you at the time: 'You'll eliminate this stuff in ten days at the most.' After eight years, some of the liquid had made its way up into your cranial passages, and some had formed a cyst in the cervical vertebrae of your neck.

It was to me that Court-Payen delivered his diagnosis: you had arachnoiditis; it was a degenerative disease and there was no cure.

I dug up thirty or so articles on myelographies, X-ray examinations of the spinal cord, that had been published in medical reviews. I wrote to the authors of some of these articles. One of them – a Norwegian, Skalpe – had conducted autopsies on humans and laboratory animals, and had shown that lipidiol is never eliminated and provokes pathologies that only grow worse with time. His letter ended with these words: 'I thank God I've never used this substance'.

The letter of a neurology professor from Baylor College of Medicine, Texas, was no more encouraging: 'Arachnoiditis is a disease in which the gossamer-like filaments covering the spinal cord as such and, sometimes, the brain, form scar tissue and compress the spinal cord as well as the roots of nerve endings going in or coming out of it. Various forms of paralysis and/or pain can result. The inhibition of certain nerves or some form of medicinal treatment may perhaps help'.

You had nothing further to hope for from medicine. You refused to get into the habit of taking analgesics and depending on them. You decided to take control of your body, your disease, your health; to seize power over your life instead of letting medical technoscience seize power over your relationship with your body, with yourself.

You got in touch with an international network of sufferers who, having coming up against the ignorance, and sometimes the resistance, of the medical profession, helped each other by exchanging information and advice. You taught yourself yoga. You took possession of yourself, body and mind, by managing your pain through ancient self-disciplines. To you, the ability to understand your suffering and take charge of yourself seemed to you to be the sole means of not being ruled by it and by the specialists who would turn you into a passive consumer of medications.

Your illness took us back to the terrain of ecology and technocriticism. My thoughts never left you when I was preparing a feature on alternative medicines for the journal. Technomedicine appeared to me to be like a particularly aggressive form of what Foucault was later to call bio-power – the power that the technological apparatus seizes, even going as far as the intimate relationship we each have with ourselves.

Two years later, we were invited a second time to Cuernavaca. We were then supposed to go on to Berkeley, then to La

Jolla, near San Diego, to Marcuse's place. You didn't notice, but I took a photo of you, from behind: you're walking with your feet in the water on the wide beach of La Jolla. You are 52 years old. You are amazing. It's one of the pictures of you that I like best.

I looked at that photo for a long while after we got back home, when you told me you wondered if you didn't have some sort of cancer. You'd already been wondering that before we left for the United States but hadn't wanted to say anything to me. Why not? 'If I have to die,' you told me calmly, 'I wanted to see California first'.

Your endometrial cancer hadn't been picked up in your annual checkup. Once the diagnosis was made and the date of the operation set, we went to spend a week in the house you'd designed. I carved your name in the stone with a chisel. That house was magic. All the spaces had a trapezoidal shape. The bedroom windows looked out over the treetops. The first night, we didn't sleep. We were both listening to each other breathing. Then a nightingale started singing and a second one, further away, started answering. We said very little to each other. I spent the day digging and looked up from time to time at the bedroom window. You'd be standing there, motionless, staring into the distance. I'm sure you were practising taming death so you could fight it without fear. You were so beautiful and so determined in your silence that I couldn't imagine you giving up living.

I took time off from the journal and shared your room at the clinic. The first night, through the open window, I heard all of Schubert's Ninth Symphony. It is etched in me, every note. I remember every moment spent at the clinic. Pierre, our doctor friend from the *Centre national de recherche scientifique,* who came to hear your latest news every morning, said to me: 'You're going through moments of exceptional intensity. You'll remember this always'.

I wanted to know what chances the oncologist gave you of surviving five years. Pierre brought me the answer: 'Fifty-fifty'.

I told myself that we should at last live in the present we shared instead of always projecting ourselves into the future. I read two books by Ursula Le Guin we'd brought back from the States. They strengthened me in this resolve.

When you came out of the clinic we went back to our house. Your spirit cheered and reassured me. You'd escaped death and life took on a new meaning and a new value. Illich immediately understood this when you saw him again a few months later, at a party. He stared into your eyes for a long time and he said to you: 'You've seen the other side.' I don't know how you responded or what else you said. But these are the words he said to me, straight afterwards: 'Those eyes! Now I understand what she means to you.'

He invited us once again to his house in Cuernavaca and added that we could stay there as long as we liked.

You'd seen 'the other side'; you'd come back from the land no one comes back from. This changed your whole outlook. Without consulting each other, we made the same resolution. An English Romantic once summed it up in a sentence: 'There is no wealth but life.'

During the months you were convalescing, I decided to take my retirement at 60. I started counting the weeks until I could pack up. I took pleasure in cooking, in tracking down organic produce that would help you get your strength back, in ordering from Wagram Place in Paris the specially tailored medications that a homeopath had recommended you take.

✳

Ecology became a way of life and a daily practice for us, although that did not stop us from feeling that what was needed was a completely different civilisation. I'd reached the age where you ask yourself what you've done with your life, what you would have liked to have done with it. I had the impression of not having *lived* my life, of having always observed it at a distance, of having developed only one side of myself and being poor as a person. You were, and always had been, richer than I was. You'd blossomed and grown in every dimension. You were at one with your life; whereas I'd always been in a hurry to move on to the next task, as though our life would only really begin later.

I asked myself what was the inessential I needed to give up so I could concentrate on the essential. I told myself that, to grasp the reach of the upheavals that were looming in every domain, there had to be more space and time for reflection than my job as a full-time journalist allowed. I didn't expect anything really innovative from the victory of the Left in 1981 and told you so after meeting two ministers from the Mauroy government the day after they were appointed.

I was amazed that my leaving the journal, after 20 years of collaboration, was painful neither to myself nor others. I remember having written to E. that, at the end of the day, only one thing was essential to me: to be with you. I can't imagine continuing to write, if you no longer are. You are the essential without which all the rest, no matter how important it seems to me when you're there, loses its meaning and its importance. I told you that in the dedication of my last work.

Twenty-three years have gone by since we went off to live in the country. First in 'your' house, with its wonderful feel of meditative harmony, a harmony we enjoyed for only three years. They started building a nuclear power station nearby and that drove us away. We found another house, very ancient, cool in summer, warm in winter, with huge grounds. It was a place where you could be happy. Where there was only a meadow, you created a garden of hedges and shrubs. I planted two hundred trees there. For a few years we still did a bit of travelling; but all the vibrating and jolting around involved in any means of transport, no matter what, triggered headaches and shooting pain through your whole body. Arachnoiditis has gradually forced you to give up most of your favourite activities. You manage to hide your suffering, though. Our friends think you're 'in great shape'.

You've never stopped encouraging me to write. Over the 23 years we've lived in the country, I've published six books and hundreds of articles and interviews. We've had dozens of visitors from every corner of the globe and I've given dozens of interviews.

It's fairly safe to say I probably haven't lived up to the resolution I made 30 years ago: to live completely at one with the present, mindful above all of the wealth of our shared life. I'm now reliving the moments when I made that resolution with a sense of urgency. I don't have any major work in the pipeline. I don't want 'to put off living till later' – in Georges Bataille's phrase – any longer. I'm as mindful of your presence now as I was in the early days and would like to make you feel that. You've given me all of your life and all of you; I'd like to be able to give you all of me in the time we have left.

You've just turned 82. You're still beautiful, graceful and desirable. We've lived together now for 58 years and I love you more than ever. Lately I've fallen in love with you all over again and I once more feel a gnawing emptiness inside that can only be filled when your body is pressed against mine.

At night I sometimes see the figure of a man, on an empty road in a deserted landscape, walking behind a hearse. I am that man. It's you the hearse is taking away. I don't want to be there for your cremation; I don't want to be given an urn with your ashes in it. I hear the voice of Kathleen Ferrier singing, 'Die Welt ist leer, Ich will nicht leben mehr'* and I wake up. I check your breathing, my hand brushes over you. Neither of us wants to outlive the other. We've often said to ourselves that if, by some miracle, we were to have a second life, we'd like to spend it together.

21 March – 6 June 2006

* The world is empty. I don't want to go on living.

André Gorz

Author, journalist and activist André Gorz was one of the leading social philosophers of the 20th century and a pioneer of political ecology. Born Gerhardt Horst in Vienna in 1923, he fled to Switzerland in 1939, a year after Austria was annexed by Nazi Germany.

He met Jean-Paul Sartre when Sartre was touring Switzerland with Simone de Beauvoir in 1946 and they remained close until the mid-1970s. A year later Gorz met the love of his life, English-born Dorine, who was working as an actress in Lausanne. Dorine was also a displaced person and an activist, equally committed to socialist ideals of rebuilding the world after the war.

Encouraged by Sartre, in 1949 the couple moved to Paris where Gorz began his career as a journalist at *Paris-Presse* under the pseudonym of Michel Bosquet. He went on to establish a fearless reputation at *L'Express* and *Le Nouvel Observateur*. But it was as André Gorz that he wrote for *Les Temps modernes*, the political, philosophical and literary magazine founded by Jean Paul Sartre and Simone de Beauvoir, and published his theoretical works.

His major works translated into English include *The Traitor; Reclaiming Work; Farewell to the Working Class; Paths to Paradise; Critique of Economic Reason; Capitalism, Socialism, Ecology; Socialism and Revolution; Ecology as Politics; The Division of Labour;* and *Strategy for Labour*. The 'Essay' Gorz referred to in *Letter to D* was finally published as *Fondements pour une morale* in 1977 by Galilée.

André Gorz's last book, *Letter to D*, was an open love letter to Dorine who was by then terminally ill. In September 2007, André and Dorine committed suicide at their country home in Vosnon, in the Aube region of France. He was 84, she was 83.

From the Translator

Lettre à D arrived on my doorstep, out of the blue, one gloomy day early in winter last year. It had been sent by Joanna Delorme at Galilée in Paris, who had published it the previous year. Joanna was offering it, she said, as a *petit cadeau* — a little present.

What a *grand cadeau* it turned out to be. I sensed that it was special the moment I began reading it, or before, as soon as I pulled it out of the padded postbag and saw the snapshot of that happy couple, on the dance floor, laughing into each other's eyes some time in the forties, causing the heart to lurch at a glance all these decades later.

I climbed into bed and read till the end, and then I lay and listened to the rain softly falling on the roses, stricken and exhilarated at the same time, as all readers of this magnificent love story must surely be.

Like the very best books, *Letter to D* will break your heart. But it also gives you a wonderful sense of how to live your life, of what matters most, of true love standing the test of time. Where have you heard that message, in such an urgent self-critical voice, coming from a married man to his wife of 58 years?

I knew I had to translate it. I felt so close to that delicate man, the woman who loved animals, the couple who truly became what they did together, that I was already trying out various English phrases as I read it the first time round. The hard part, I knew, would be to 'nail' that distinctive voice — the voice of truth, rare and particular, full of love yet free of any sentimentality.

I've translated a lot of books from Galilée, difficult, elaborate books by France's leading intellectuals. This was harder than any of them, in a way. It is so simple on the surface, so tight, yet so emotionally complex, that the tiniest false note rings out like a gong.

Gorz isn't just any man in love, either. In France, he's a household name in the field of philosophy and politics. Sartre called him the most intelligent man in Paris at a time when that was really saying something. A friend of mine, now the head of a French governmental organisation, told me Gorz taught him everything he knew about socialism and ecology.

There are passages in this tale that make difficult demands on an audience less familiar with the history of ideas in postwar France, when it was great to be young and alive and an intellectual in the capital of Europe, if not the world. In France the book was an overnight success and sold out fast. Gorz, who modestly suggested a print run of a few thousand copies, was amazed when it became a bestseller.

It wasn't until last September, when A and D's 'pact for 'life' carried on into eternity, where they now lie in an inseparable embrace after carrying out the suicide pact we sense hovering at the end of *Letter to D*, that their story spread to the English-speaking world. I was commissioned to translate an extract for a British newspaper and other extracts also appeared in Britain. Publishers around the world began bidding for foreign rights, moved to tears by the articles they'd read.

I'd like to thank Fiona Henderson, my editor at HarperCollins Australia, for her passionate insight into the book and her fabulous ear; and my wonderful friend, Joanna Delorme, for the beauty of her gift.

JR

Sydney

February 2008

Notes for the Reader

Günther **Anders**: (1902–1992) German philosopher, journalist, essayist and anti-nuclear activist. Born in Breslau, he lived in Paris and the US in the 1930s and in Vienna from the mid-1950s. Major work: *The Outdatedness of Human Beings* (1956).

Charles **Apothéloz**: (1922–1982) Leading light in the theatre scene of French-speaking Switzerland, avant-garde theatre director, founder of *Compagnie des Faux Nez* (Company of the False Noses) and later director of the Lausanne State Theatre.

Georges **Bataille**: (1897–1962) Writer, anthropologist and philosopher known as 'the metaphysician of evil'. Major works: *On Nietzsche* (1945), *Theory of Religion* (1948), *Literature and Evil* (1957), *The Tears of Eros* (1961), *The Impossible* (1962).

Simone de **Beauvoir**: (1908–1986) Philosopher, novelist, essayist and feminist who developed with Jean-Paul Sartre the theory of existentialism. Major works: *The Second Sex* (1949), *The Blood of Others* (1945), *The Mandarins* (1954), *Memoirs of a Dutiful Daughter* (1958), *The Prime of Life* (1960), *Force of Circumstance* (1963), *A Very Easy Death* (1964) *The Woman Destroyed* (1967). She is referred to in *Letter to D* only by her nickname, Castor.

Jane **Birkin**: (b.1946) British-born actress, singer and film director, a longtime resident of France.

Maurice **Blanchot**: (1907–2003) Writer and literary theorist Blanchot was a close friend of Georges Bataille. Major works: *Death Sentence* (1948), *The Book to Come* (1959*)*, *The Writing of the Disaster* (1980), *A Voice From Elsewhere* (2002).

Kazimierz **Brandys**: (1916–2000) Polish novelist and journalist who lived in France from 1970. *The*

Defence of Grenada Gorz refers to is a short story by Brandys.

Bread and Roses: A left-wing wing arm of an American women's movement formed in the 1930s to represent working women.

Albert **Camus**: (1913–1960) Philosopher, novelist, essayist, journalist. Born in Algeria, Camus moved to France in 1938 and was active in the Resistance during the Occupation. He became a columnist for the newspaper, *Combat*, and its chief editor from 1943. He was awarded the Nobel Prize for Literature in 1957 for his contribution to literature, theatre and philosophy. Camus' *The Outsider* (*L'Étranger* 1942) Gorz refers to is one of the best-known examples of absurdist fiction. Other major works include *The Myth of Sisyphus* (1942), *The Plague* (1947), *The Fall* (1956), *Exile and the Kingdom* (1957). Camus was killed in a car accident at the age of 47.

Jean-Yves **Calvez**: (b.1927) Author of *La pensée de Karl Marx* (The Thoughts of Karl Marx) published in 1956.

Castor, **Sartre and the 'family'**: The members of the editorial board of the monthly review, *Les Temps modernes*, founded by Jean-Paul Sartre and Simone de Beauvoir in 1945. Gorz joined them in 1962, forming an 'inner circle' of familiars, the so-called 'family'. Castor, meaning 'beaver', was Simone de Beauvoir's nickname.

CFDT: *Confédération française démocratique du travail* (French Democratic Confederation of Work) One of the strongest of the five main trade union groups in France.

CNRS: *Centre national de recherche scientifique* (National Centre of Scientific Research). Established in 1939, the centre's postwar mission was the support and funding of scientific and general university research.

Citizens of the World: A movement founded by American peace activist Garry Davis (b.1921) after the Second World War. Its aim was to abolish nation states and form a world state instead, with a global constitution, a world parliament and a world government. It reached its high point in late 1948, when a proclamation issued by Citizens of the World was read out at a United Nations General Assembly calling for 'one government for one world'. Prominent supporters included Albert Camus, André Breton and the Abbé Pierre.

Jean **Daniel**: (b.1920) Novelist and journalist. Worked at *L'Express* with Gorz before leaving to become co-founder and chief editor of the news review *Le Nouvel Observateur* in 1964, under the patronage of Pierre Mendès-France and Jean-Paul Sartre.

Gilles **Deleuze**: (1925–1995) French philosopher who wrote many influential works on philosophy, literature, film and fine art. Major works: the two volumes of *Capitalism and Schizophrenia: Anti-Oedipus* (1972) and *A Thousand Plateaus* (1980), both co-written with Félix Guattari.

Isaac **Deutscher** (1907–1967) British journalist, historian and political activist of Polish-Jewish birth. He became well known as the biographer of Leon Trotsky and Joseph Stalin and as a commentator on Soviet affairs.

Marcel **Duhamel**: (1900–1977) Creator and editor of the legendary *'Série noire'* crime series with French publisher, Gallimard.

Jacques **Ellul**: (1912–1994) Protestant theologian and anarchist, philosopher, socialist and a professor at Bordeaux University. One of the most influential critics of technology as a dehumanising process, he argued that machines cancel out humanity's accumulated memory, knowledge, skills and faith.

Major works include *The Technological Society* (1964), *The New Demons* (1973), *The Betrayal of the West* (1975), *The Political Illusion* (1977) and *What I Believe* (1987).

François **Erval**: (1914–1999) Journalist and publisher. Co-founder, with Maurice Nadeau, of the literary periodical, *La Quinzaine littéraire*, which first appeared in 1979.

André **Gide** (1869–1951) French author and Nobel Prize winner. He explored themes of sexual freedom, social equality and atheism in his writing, including his journals, which were later published. He won the Nobel Prize for literature in 1947.

Tiennot **Grumbach**: Co-founder of the libertarian group *Vive la Révolution* (VLR) in 1968. Later founded his own law firm, which exclusively represents wage-earners and trade unions in legal disputes.

La Gueule ouverte (The Open Mouth) An ecological journal published in 1972.

Pierre-Félix **Guattari**: (1930–1992) French militant, institutional psychotherapist and philosopher, founder of both schizoanalysis and ecosophy. Guattari is best known for his intellectual collaborations with Gilles Deleuze, most notably *Anti-Oedipus* (1972) and *A Thousand Plateaus* (1980).

Ivan **Illich**: (1926–2002) Essayist, philosopher and teacher. An early exponent of liberation theology, Illich was a cult figure of the 1970s counterculture for his work on 'counter productivity' and as an environmentalist. Major works include *Deschooling Society* (1971), *Tools for Conviviality* (1973), *Medical Nemesis* (1978).

Jean **Jaurès**: (1859–1914) Socialist politician and one of the best-known representatives of democratic socialism in France in his time. A passionate pacifist and republican, he was shot dead by a young nationalist in the Café du Croissant, Paris, shortly before the outbreak of the First World War.

Francis **Jeanson**: (b.1922) Philosopher, author and editor at *Les Temps modernes*.

Robert **Laponche**: Physicist and expert on sustainable energy. Colleague and scientific advisor to Michel Rolant (see overleaf).

Ursula **Le Guin** (b.1929) Award-winning American science-fiction writer.

Benny **Lévy**: (1945–2003) Philosopher and writer, and one-time secretary to Sartre. From the early 1970s, he led a small Maoist group, 'Gauche prolétarienne' (GP), set up by journalist Serge July in 1969. Lévy also edited the group's newspaper, *La Cause du peuple*.

Claude **Lévi-Strauss**: (b.1908) Ethnologist and anthropologist, founder of Structuralism. Major works: *The Elementary Structures of Kinship* (1949), *Tristes tropiques* (1955), *Structural Anthropology* (1958), *The Savage Mind* (1962), *Totemism* (1962), *Structural Anthropology II* (1973) and *Look, Listen, Read* (1993).

Herbert **Marcuse**: (1898–1979) German political theorist and teacher. Born in Berlin, he became a US citizen in 1940 and went on to become a cult figure of the student left, with his analysis of new forms of social control and technological domination. Major works: *Eros and Civilisation* (1955), *One-Dimensional Man* (1964).

Pierre **Mauroy**: (b.1928) Socialist politician and Prime Minister of France under President François Mitterand, from 1981–1984.

Pierre **Mendès France**: (1907–1982) Prime Minister of France (1954–1955), statesman and diplomat. Minister of the Economy in the interim government of 1944, then a radical Democrat opponent of Charles de Gaulle. The phrase 'lifeblood of the nation' comes from a speech he addressed to the youth of France in December 1955, encouraging political involvement.

Maurice **Merleau-Ponty**: (1908–1961) Major philosopher and phenomenologist, collaborated on *Les Temps modernes*, though he later broke with Simone de Beauvoir and Jean-Paul Sartre. Major works: *The Structure of Behaviour* (1942), *Phenomenology of Perception* (1945), *Humanism and Terror* (1947) and *Sense and Non-Sense* (1948).

Our Bodies, Our Selves: A cult reference book on women's health and sexuality, issued by the American collective of the same name. It first appeared in 1973 and was translated into more than 20 languages.

Michel **Rolant**: (1936–1995) A strategist for the *Confédération française démocratique du travail* (CFDT) and member of the executive committee from 1982 in charge of energy policy. Founder of the trade union for nuclear industry workers and a strong critic of the French nuclear program.

Romain **Rolland**: (1866–1944) Writer and pacifist. Awarded the Nobel Prize for Literature in 1915. Best-known works: the 10-volume *Jean-Christophe* (1904-1912) and *Above the Fray*, justifying his silence over the Dreyfus Affair, which split French society.

Jean-Paul **Sartre**: (1905–1980) Philosopher, writer, novelist, playwright, teacher and bone fide 'politically engaged' intellectual. Wrote his philosophical masterwork, *Being and Nothingness*, in 1943, which was the basis of existentialism, founded with lifelong partner Simone de Beauvoir in 1945. Founded the magazine *Les Temps modernes* with Beauvoir in 1945. Became active from 1968 in various left-wing movements. Major works: *Nausea* (1938), *The Flies* (1943), *Being and Nothingness* (1943), *The Road to Freedom trilogy (The Age of Reason,* 1945; *The Reprieve,* 1947; *Iron in the Soul,* 1949*), Dirty Hands (*1948), *The Devil and the Good Lord* (1951), *Saint Genet, Actor and Martyr* (1952), *The Condemned of Altona* (1959), *Critique of Dialectical Reason* (1960), *The Words* (1964) and *The Family Idiot* (on Gustave Flaubert) (1971-2).

Jean-Jacques **Servan-Schreiber**: (JJSS, 1924–2006) Journalist and essayist, founder of the left liberal news magazine, *L'Express*, with Françoise Giroud, in 1953. Closely associated with Mendès France, he fought to oppose Charles de Gaulle.

Sauvage: Bi-monthly ecological magazine, in which Gorz published many of the articles that would form part of *Ecology As Politics* (1975).

The Traitor: Andre Gorz's first published book. The primary focus of *The Traitor* is Gorz's intensive and extensive deployment of 'theory' (Marxist, psychoanalytic and existentialist) as a way of comprehending the self and its situation. Gorz depicted himself and Dorine through the book's key characters.

UNESCO: The United Nations Educational, Scientific and Cultural Organisation founded in November 1945 to promote education, communication and the arts.